The Double Witness

Library of Congress Cataloging in Publication Data will
be found on the last printed page of this book

Publication of this book has been aided by a grant from the
Paul Mellon Fund at Princeton University Press

This book has been composed in Linotype Monticello

Printed in the United States of America
by Princeton University Press, Princeton, New Jersey

ACKNOWLEDGMENTS

I am grateful to the following publications for permission to reprint the poems
listed below:

Modern Poetry Studies: "Boiling the Egg," "Nighttown: Block Island"
The New Yorker: "Xerox," "Soundings," and an abbreviated version of "A
    Suicide: Paran Creek"
Poetry: "Full Moon: The Gorge"
Salmagundi: "'Ah, Sunflower!'," "Freshwater Pond," "A Choppy Sea,"
    "From the Firehouse," "This Scribe, My Hand"
The Sewanee Review: "The Guanajuato Mummies," "The Repellant"
The Southern Review: "An Orange in Mérida," "Cat's Cradle"
The Virginia Quarterly Review: "Kites," "Swan Lake," "Glare," "Southeast
    Lighthouse," "The Double-Goer"

Two poems from NOWHERE BUT LIGHT and one translation from the
Appendix to Antonio Machado's JUAN DE MAIRENA have also been in-
cluded in the belief that they are indispensable to the "doublings" and "soli-
tudes" to which these poems bear "witness," and complete the design of this
volume. My thanks are due the University of Chicago Press for permission to
reprint "Block Island Crossing" and "Fat Tuesday," and to the University of
California Press for "The Journey of Abel Martín."

                                                                        B.B.

. . . this want of witness in brute nature . . .
—GERARD MANLEY HOPKINS
Letter to W. R. Dixon

. . . reckon but, reck but, mind
But these two; ware of a world where but these two tell, each off
the other . . .
—*Spelt From Sibyl's Leaves*
GERARD MANLEY HOPKINS

Table of Contents

Xerox

The original man lies down to be copied
face down on glass. He thinks what it is
to be other than he was, while the pilot light
goes garnet, a salamander's eye
blinks in the camera's cave, green burns like the skin
of the water seen by a surfacing swimmer,
and the moving and shaking begin.

What must it be, to be many? thinks the singular
man. Underneath, in the banked fluorescence, the rollers
are ready. A tarpaulin falls. A humming of flanges
arises, a sound like rail meeting rail
when power slams out of the fuses. A wick explodes
in the gases—and under the whole of his length
the eye of the holocaust passes.

And all that was lonely, essential, unique
as a fingerprint, is doubled. Substance and essence,
the mirror and the figure that printed the mirror,
the deluge that blackened creation and the hovering pigeon
with the leaf's taste in its beak,
are joined. The indivisible sleeper is troubled;
What does it mean to be legion?

he cries in the hell of the copied. The rapists, the lovers,
the stealers of blessings, the corrupt and derivative
devils, whirl over the vacant emulsion.
The comedian peers from the brink and unsteadily copies
its laughter. The agonist prints its convulsion.
Like turns to like, while the seminal man on the glass
stares at his semblance and calls from the pit of the ink:

3

Swan Lake

The swan, a stylist, born to the posture of the question mark
and the bishop's mitre—
balletic, episcopal, unsentimental,
a hater of Tchaikowsky, inadvertently
settling his calm posterior like a tutu, fixing his seedy
eyeball like a lorgnette in the garbage and crumbs—
is nobody's accompanist. He leads
a hard flotilla in half a V,
parting the cattails, makes a fist
of his breastbone, aims the carroty wax of his beak,
and smashes the flat of the pond
till nothing is seen in the scum
but the doubled hose and the albino spur of his rump.

Never having read
Ovid's *Metamorphoses*, he is content
with the basic changes of the uxorious loner:
his cygnets making chevrons in the swamp,
training for puberty, drifting like crumpled carbon paper
with the letters showing faintly through the smudge,
pica on elite,
till white burns through the hump
and all that was ordinary turns exceptional.

The swan is unreflective, opposing the hard outline
to the blur,
casting a classical image like the Parthenon
in an Ionian ambiguity of pomp,
oblivious to imagery, equivalent
only to itself. Those who have known his anger,
know the alternate sides of a coin: tenderness
and homicidal hate—
the beer-drinking family man, and the fighter
cocked with a trigger's violence,
showing the naked triangle of his uvula
parted to the gullet under a bony bulb, like the Guernica horses—

as the whole contrivance hisses and advances,
saying:
   Bastards! Bastards! Bastards!
         —and tacks round
and stands its ground.

Double Poem of the World's Burning

1. "Ah, Sunflower!"

Preparing for that presence, the pod
chose a man's height, set its cleats in the leaves
like a steeplejack, scribbled its target of ovals,
and rose to eye level.

Climbing a profile of gardens, a Nimzo-Indian
chessboard of vegetables, villages, rock with its pollen
of lichen, the sunflower steadied its petals in zodiacal
yellow, and struck like a clock.

All the world's plenty, all the brazen particulars—a bull's-eye
of seeds with the pips pointing down into chain-metal, an obsidian
disk bulging with roe like a carp—took on the hardness
of Chinese enamels

and opened its perfect meniscus. Then the terrible
heaviness began—the failing of bronzes, the hasp at the sunflower's
center breaking away, a fading of planets, eclipses, coronas,
the falling and falling away of the petals—

Time's total weariness, the terrible weight in the sun—all
that hammers at darkness and glows like the baize of the table
    Van Gogh
saw at Arles in the cornfields and candles, a madman painting the
    night till
the sky was delivered again to the crows.

10

2. *Glare: Atlacomulco*

And His raiment was white as the light.

The invisible life that sleeps in the grossness of things
and feeds on the bulk of the world
bringing substance and weight and degree—

the tumescence
that traces a thread in the loins, to the swamp
of our human duration

and insists on the blood and the bone of our presence—
shows the world's burning,
turned low, like the flame in the bell of a lamp.

Blue as acetylene, it waits
at the furthest edge of the morning, a transparency
holding a bird and a steely horizon:

the water repeats it, gunmetal on pewter,
pewter on ultramarine,
doubling the universe, spilling the colors

and shapes of a season
on the rubble and flint of a planet, crowding
the leaf to its uttermost margin, filling the spaces,

till nothing is latent, nothing withheld or unnameable:
the spike of the cactus, the fuse in the tulipan, the sun
at its zenith, lie flat on the plane of the sky like an armorer's anvil,

11

yes, love's ignominious reversals that my heart's starvation
would have reversed if it could: night with its names for powers,
dominations, fears: houses, Homeric fictions: Dante astray
in the tiger-taken wood: Hell with its vortical vengeances:
and night, night without respite or guile, the light of common day.

An Orange in Mérida

The orange-peelers of Mérida, in the wrought-
iron midday, come with mechanical skewers
and live oranges, to straddle the paths
on caissons of bicycle wheels
and work in the dark of the plaza, like jewelers' cloths,

The orange, they say, is ceremonious.
Its sleep is Egyptian. Its golden umbilicus
waits in pyramidal light, swath over swath, outwitting
the Caesars. It cannot be ravaged by knives,
but clasps its mortality in, like the skein of an asp.

The bandstand glitters like bone, in laurel
and spittle. Behind their triangular
catafalques, the orange-peelers move through the thirst
of the world with Rameses' bounty
caulked into the hive of the peel

while ratchets and wheels spin a blazing
cosmology on their little machines. Under
skewers and handles, the orange's skin
is pierced, the orange, in chain mail and papyrus,
unwinds the grave clothes of Pharaoh

in a helix of ribbon, unflawed, from the navel's
knot to the rind and the pulp underneath, like a butterfly's
chrysalis. And sleeper by sleeper, the living turn with their thirst
to each other, the orange's pith is broken
in a blind effervescence that perfumes the palate and burns

to the tooth's bite. And the dead reawaken.

We are wracked with the pangs of our fasting. We are alive.
The children approach us with sugary ribbons:
"A mummy, señor?" they say. And they offer us candy.

Mocking, solicitous, the children insist. The children wait to be paid.

We bite through the skulls in the cellophane wrappers.

We burn in the sunlight, afraid.

II. FROM THE FIREHOUSE

The Old Firehouse, just across the street from the new, on Paran Creek in North Bennington, Vermont, served as studio for Paul Terence Feeley, the gifted American painter, until his untimely death in 1965, when it was converted into a storehouse for his canvases and a residence for his wife; and more recently, a sub-let for friends.

From the Firehouse
(Homage to Paul Feeley)

Living between two fires and two falls—a stairway
of watery risers and treads above and below, holding
the fish to its floor and the foam to the swallow's
intaglio, an old Firehouse and a new—I think only
of canvas, like a Bedouin. Now in the whimsical
playground of your cellar, that birthday-box of aerial toys,
beginning with the color red, as children do,
I listen for engines folding their ladders in a burst
of exploding bells, a village in its underdrawers
wakened by the color red, from its dream of sexual famine:
colors that bound from the canvas like a rubber ball
in a rite of counted jack-rocks, Cyclopean maces, panels
and chess pawns—your Euclidean signature, Paul.

And all night hear a skip-rope slapping canvas
between the crated sculpture and the mildewing gravel
where your boxer-father dances, shedding the color red,
lashing a corner of the Engine Room with his dream of travel
that flings you toward the Spanish littoral and flings
you back, shedding the color red, mortal Moroccan red.
I build a house as you would build in cards or canvas,
with a gambler's riffle of whiskey and aces in spades,
or as your Damascan namesake built with a tent of
flames and sizing dazzled with lights and voices,
painting your contemptuous apotheosis of guilt
with a jeweler's balances, thumb to the palette
like a bowling ball, breaking a string of shapes and reassembling
the shapes in identical frames to demolish the spaces.

21

Trout-hunter, dawdling in feathers and flies, land-sailor
skewed to an Irish passion for magnified miniatures,
miniature magnitudes—alternative symmetries
of the old wood-worshipers building with megaliths or
lacing the finical borders of the Book of Kells—bending your forms
with the precarious delineation of metal hammered thin:
fastidious, prayerful illuminator: the dream
on the Firehouse floor is not for you, beached for the night
like a clipper under gauzes and tarpaulins and butcher's papers.
I cannot bear the striking of your colors, that Sargasso of
passionate forms. But sometimes from your sun deck I have seen
a crazy armada, canvas over canvas, break a storm
of sails, climb the stair to the millrace and the esplanade
of barns, burn with Egyptian extravagance in the maples
and window-glass, tacking toward Cydnus to call you from the dead
and paint our northern autumn with Pompeian red.

Cat's Cradle

Something the cat watches from his
cradle, in Ishmael's image,
his ear laid lightly
in swatches of cross-hairs, like a
marksman sighting
a target of silence, the circuits ᵢ
of a stethoscope's medallion,
looks back at the cat in midsummer
lightning and waits at a hole in the dark.

Something cavernous, cloacal, rank,
like a breathing of grills in a sewer
or a failed
stem in a glass
that thickened into mucus and then
stank; the frog on the well's floor, winy
with compost, ringed with ovulation;
the sac in the prawn's side, gorged;
the leaven in the whale's lump and the slime.

Dilating or sheathing his claws,
whiskered and spiked
like a Hapsburg, paws to his
ruff, with his eye-hairs
hiked in a vector, paring time
with his eye-slits,
the cat from his crow's nest
on the creek bank,
predatory, tactical, binocular,

genius of speculation, feels
for a cause in the dark—
slippage of glaciers
and Precambrian corings, a
sleepwalking pigeon
shifting his stance or his feathers,
the mouse's tooth in a platen
of marrow, jeweled
on a hairspring of leather: feels

with the whole of his instinct,
dinosaur and serpent diminishing
to a purr—the whole
encompassment of darkness, invisible
ripenings like the bloom
on the underside of a leaf, darkness's
mother wit rising and falling, the boughs' subtle
breathing where noon is the thickest—whether to
magnify being or make our nullity rich:

the cat will tell you which.

(For Jack Moore)

24

A Suicide: Paran Creek

*Cleopatra: Give me my Robe, put on my Crowne, I have
Immortall longings in me.*

The granny glasses under
their blind earpieces
folded over, the untimely cobalt
coat, quartered
into itself, and the painful
cane in the starved
March grass—put by
in decorous self-murder—

everything seemed urgent—

even the scum on the creek bank
where the millrace
smoked under flotsam
smelling of horsepiss, sour lumber,
detergent—

as, punctual to a fault,
you stayed to look your last
at the ordered street light, cropped
like a crozier, the Firehouse clock
in the car barn
with its cunning pageantry of hoses,
its ambulance in yogurt and enamel—
that might suddenly shriek,
whirl in a carousel—bells, or
blood-roses—

and with no hope
of manageable disaster—

25

you leaned to a muddy bottom,
all your length, face
down, as you would read
a hieroglyph of cancer and arthritis
and acedia, and left a floating answer
in the morning.

> *Yet something warmed you strangely*
> *for a moment—a midsummer trick of swallows*
> *over water, the trout's*
> *whiplash under a shaking rainbow,*
> *a black cat on the newspapers*
> *and comics where a child*
> *bought licorice strings—*

> *or the "immortal longings"*
> *of a sister who wore*
> *Seleucid's stolen*
> *bangle under her pharaoh's robe,*
> *flinched in contrary cold: "Your*
> *crown's awry; I'll mend it*
> *and then play—"*

while you, her diffident neighbor,
alike in longing,
faced the other way at one
or two in the morning, hard
hearted, anachronistic,
put off your steaming glasses
in Alexandrian blood-heat,
the blue, unseasonable coat, and
the cane beside them—just
as your note foretold—
and were delivered down.

26

The Double-Goer
(North Bennington)

1.

Seeing that dangerous mover,
we remembered the hazards of walking, again:
the mastodon's trick
of stacking his spine on its child's box of blocks;
the mantis's walking stick;
or the equilibrist
bearing down with the webs and the soles of his feet,
claw over crystal, and printing a town with his fists,
isometric, saurian, prehensile,
moving toward plunder.

2.

Face to face
with that obdurate profile pointed one way only,
drawn to its length like a bowstring,
with the noose
of a tie underneath, and a hatband
to level his jaw to the set of his teeth,
an arrowhead flinty with mourning,
insomniac, lonely—
coming or going we averted our glance when we met
and offered our backs to our guilt.

God help our uneasy walkers, we said: God hold
their weight to the invisible wheel
of their feet driving their anguish uphill
in all weathers; tether
their toes to the chains
moving over and under, tighten
the tendons and ratchets:
God true their purchase,
walking past taverns and graveyards in a hemorrhage
of leaves or the herringbone blue
of the snow. Make their placelessness perfect, going
nowhere, wherever they go.

3.

Where should a man walk in his fear and his need?
The gymnopede
walks out of his innocence into his vertigo,
rises and falls on his toes,
knowing all distance is mortal, all walking
demonic. The wanderer, trying his exile over and over,
measures his failing humanity,
and the stalker intending him harm
circles the sufferer, crumbles a spoor with his fingers,
and walks toward the print of his prey.

Only the walker keeps earthen.
The saltimbanque,
tumbling toward God, falls another way. The swimmer
working in fathoms, the breaker of ether,
alter their stance to their element
and forsake the old Adam. What was vertical,
durative, perishing,
falls like a diver, or floats on a stilled horizontal.
Only the walker totters past the rattles and mats
of his childhood, erect, toward the sexual flaw
of his symmetry, goes frontal
and doubles his burden.

4.

Even pity is helpless. Should we question
the bartering God—supposing
all action were fable, all
being, beginning: a "prologue in Heaven"
or a charade for two players
bent over their pawns,
the unmoved movers of a dice-cup shaken by good and evil:
should we ask, midway in the walk:

"Why go looking for trouble? Why
lengthen your distance to hate us? Where do you walk?
Where are you from?"
—the answer already is given,
Belial's or Baudelaire's: *"From
going to and fro in the earth and from walking up and down
in it.* I am your Adversary,
homicidal or prodigal, Dutchman
or equivocal Jew, practising life: I am Ishmael,
your brother, your double, your Other."

III. SOLITUDES

(Homage to Antonio Machado)

Antonio Machado (1875-1939), Spain's greatest master of the "Generation of '98," lived out a widower's life of deprival as teacher of French in high schools at Baeza, Soria, and Segovia, and died in exile in France toward the close of the Spanish Civil War. Among his final works is a volume of "apocryphal poems" and a collection of prose "epigrams, maxims, memoranda, and memoirs" of an "apocryphal professor" in whose guises as Meneses, Mairena, and Martín he disclosed the erotic and philosophical preoccupations of a lifetime.

Fat Tuesday

Yesterday's
seven-thirty still clots the bandstand
clock. A child sleeps near the tinsel and papier maché
in a kerosene ring under the wavering flies.
The lovers embrace on the grandstand

as slowly
the machinery of celebration engages
its spokes and wheels around the incandescent center
of their pleasure. The plazas sparkle like stages
with a blind bicarbonation, and the masquers enter.

How simply
their dangerous reversal
is accomplished, the permutations of concealment
turning the cheesecloth and the mica of their disguises
into the dramatis personae of a dress rehearsal

and showing
the eye-hole's razor edges framing the double ovals
of the masquer's eyes, like buckets re-arising in a well, glowing
with vagrant spontaneities, the amateur's surprises
caught in the act of his improvisations.

Knowing
those Tuesdays of the flesh, reptilian
in their hungers, Antonio Machado, dragging his horsehair
greatcoat, his *Irregular Verbs for French Beginners*, the chalky
bastinado of his calling,

through the parched
Castilian school day, in earshot of a parish's explosion,
scribbled a maxim in his *Marginalia*:
"Not to put on one's mask, but to put off one's face: that
is Carnival. The face alone in the world—that is appalling!"

And watched
from a cindery tussock how the masquers circled
a fountain in Baeza, putting off his cheekbones, eyes, the sensuous
underlip, emptying his skull of what it held
under the make-believe regalia,

leaving only
the arm-band of the widower's long deprival,
the schoolteacher who had "studied under Bédier and Bergson"
counting martlets between the bell-tower and horizon,
intent on the apocryphal and lonely.

And noted:
"The poet is a fisher in time: not of fish
in the sea, but the whole living catch: let us be clear about that!"
He put off his face, facing away from Madrid. The Tuesday of the
    guns grew fat.
He crossed the border into France, put on his mask and died into
    his wish.

Boiling the Egg

"Poetry is the word in its time; and students of poetry must maximize the temporality of their verse . . . All our class exercises have been devoted to this end. . . . I especially remember a poem called Boiling the Egg."

—JUAN DE MAIRENA

On that morning of his exile,
there was a sound of gunshot and zarzuelas from a nondescript
cantina. He looked toward Soria and Segovia, comedian
of the grieving countenance, packed his bag for France, and scoured
    his table-top
like an apothecary

to boil an egg. All
was in readiness: the mourners and personae of a lifetime—Meneses
and Mairena and Martín—the pestle and the mortar
of a broken boyhood, his widower's thirst, with its bucket on a rachet
by the well, and a wheel

to draw his dearth up
from the cypresses and solitude of Castile—and for his last vagary,
the battered barber's basin of a hero, sand from the Caves of
    Montesinos
to measure off the minutes of his hourglass; and the egg
shaped like a zero.

He lighted his spirit lamp,
candled his whimsical egg, as for some feat of prestidigitation,
turned back his watch dial's fatal circuit to cancel out
the day, climbed the college ramp to erase a pedant's quibble—
    "*Dasein* into *Néant* into *Nada*—"
and began his peroration:

"That we must wait until the egg
boils or the door opens or the cucumber ripens is
something that merits your reflection, gentlemen!" The listeners
  drew closer.
"Democritus moves the atoms in the Universal Egg; but the boiling
  of the water
is the work of Heraclitus. It is

irreversible." And yet, how easily the boy
from Chipiona might have sucked that egg, blown out its white
  and yolk
through a pinhole in the shell, filled the void with perfume or confetti,
circled the circling lovers in the six-o'clock *paseo*, and smashed
the oval on a darkening carnival!

The egg boiled on, with none to see
the bloodlines in a map of Europe hardening in albumen,
the yolk melt down the crown of Montezuma, the caciques
of Isabella drink the steam up like a mushroom, Hiroshima's
  tissue-paper
skies catch fire in the conflagration.

He waited till the needle
splintered the spindle in his hourglass and the lingering bubbles
  ran to froth.
Only the egg remained, unscathed and disimagined, in the burning.
Then he pinched the blueing flame with a forefinger, dinted the
  egg's perfection,
and moved forth on his journey.

36

Journey of Abel Martín

1.

Circling the bell-tower,
the martlets, trailing, soar:
children are storming the air and crying at their wars.
Adept in his solitude, Martín, in a corner there.
Evening or twilight making, dust,
and a squabble of voices, a child's vociferations—
fifty or twelve, however you make it, all's one.

O starveling spirit and prodigal of soul,
by the glowering bonfire's circle
where dead sticks crackle in a fiery air
and blazon a blind frontier,
showing its blackest cicatrices clear!

The living shall surely perish, as Abel said.
Ah, distance, distance! the star
that none may handle, yet lightens the way ahead:
shall any voyage prosper, lacking it?

Great eye that looks on distance—O lessening sail!
heart indurate in absence,
bland herbs
and honeys of love, blessed in forgetfulness.
Lore of the mastering Zero, of the rounded
fruit's quintessence ripening for man's need,
gout that breaks in a dream, and fountainhead of shadow,
shadow of godhead under the stretched, dread hand!
Before, it be Day, if day be given, indeed,
the all-beholding light that is not yet come to pass,
whelm what is vile in me, outcry and exhortation,
Lord of all essences, and drown me in Nothingness!

37

2.

And that angel, skilled
in his secret, went out to Martín in the pass.
He gave him the little he had—the pietist's
pittance, perhaps? or a sop for extortionists?
Perhaps. But Martín there in the cold
knew himself lonely, strove with his knowledge, reproved
the Omnipotent Knower Who had no eye for His child,
and all that night in unspeakable wilderness moved.

3.

And saw his equivocal Muse
erect by his bedstead, the fugitive
haunting his streets, the bereft
and impossible love and the lady forever beloved.
And called to her: Lady,
for the uncovering of that face, my passion
thought to live until morning
though my heart's blood turn to suet.
Wisdom is given me now. You are other than I dreamt.
Yet would I bless you still
and gaze the more, however you walked at your will
at my side, in cold contempt.
                              Death turned to smile
at Martín, but knew no way to do it.

4.

I lived, I drowsed, I dreamed—
Martín thought, while his pupils thickened—
and thereby conceived a man in a slumbering vigil
intent on his dream, beyond what is dreamt or imagined.
Yet, if a harder reckoning be wanting,
equal for dreamer and watcher alike, and the same
for those who apportion the roads
and those who follow them, panting,
conception in perfect nullity is yours, in the end:
the shadow of your presence, a colossus,
divinity left gazing at us blinded.

5.

First anguish; then exhaustion,
the pangs of despairing assurance:
the unappeasable thirst no water may ever diminish,
wormwood of time made poisonous with durance.
That lyre stretched for his dying!

                            Abel made trial with his hand
of his emaciate body.
Beholder of all that exists, did His vision not see him there, lying?
O the sloth of it, bleeding oblivion!

Help me, Lord help me!

                            His life, from its beginnings,
the unchangeable fable of his being, hovered,
traced on the yielding wax.
Would he melt with the coming of day in the sun?
Abel lifted a hand
to the light
of the vehement morning reddening into summer
that burned on the balcony of his dimming habitation.
Blinded, he groped for the glimmer he had never discovered.
Then he raised to his lips,
grown icier now, unhurried, the immaculate glass
of purest dark—O purest darkness!—brimming.

(*After Antonio Machado*)

41

IV. THIS SCRIBE, MY HAND

This living hand, now warm and capable
Of earnest grasping . . . see, here it is—
I hold it towards you.
    —JOHN KEATS

This Scribe, My Hand

When this warm scribe, my hand, is in the grave.
—JOHN KEATS

1.

You are here
on the underside of the page,
writing in water,

anachronist,
showing your head
with its delicate fuses,

its fatal telemetry,
a moundful of triggers and gunpowder
like a field-mine,

your sixty-one inches
and your gem cutter's fingers,
anonymous,

taking the weight
of a "roomful of people"
but making no mark,

pressing the page as I write,
while the traffic in Rome
demotic with engines and klaxons

circles the Pyramid of Cestius,
crosses a graveyard, and submerges
again like the fin of a shark.

2.

I write, in the posthumous way,
on the flat of a headstone
with a quarrier's ink, like yourself:

an anthologist's date and an asterisk,
a parenthetical mark in the gas
of the pyramid-builders,

an obelisk whirling with Vespas
in a poisonous motorcade.
I make your surgeon's incision for

solitude—one living hand, two
poets strangled in sea-water and phlegm,
an incestuous

ego to reach for
the heart in the funeral ashes,
a deathbed with friends.

3.

Something murderous flows
from the page to my hand—
a silence that wars

with the letters, a fist
that closes on paper: a blow
with the straight edge of a razor

that falls with a madman's
monotony, or the adze
of a sleepwalking Sumerian

nicking the wet of the clay,
hacking a wedge in a tablet
in the blood and the mica,

till all glistens with language.
The criminal folds up his claspknife. The shutters
slam down on the streets. Nobody listens.

4.

Out of breath with the climb, and
tasting a hashish of blood,
what did he see on the brink

of the Piazza di Spagna? A hand
in the frame of a cithara
where beggars and sunbathers

clotted the levels like musical
signatures, a Wordsworthian
dream of degree, unimaginable

time touched by an axe
blade—or a pram
on the Steps of Odessa

torn from the hands of
its mother, gathering speed for the
plunge and rocking its tires

in the rifling, like a gun barrel,
smashing its way through the Tzar's
executioners, to a scream at the bottom?

5.

A failed solitude. The bees
in the Protestant grass
speak of it delicately

in the sweat of a
Palatine summer, guiding my hand
through the Braille of the letters.

Violet, bluet, or squill—
what was it I picked
under the epitaph, what

rose to my touch
in the thirst of the marble, a cup
from the well of your grave

in the noonday miasma,
a hieroglyph in the water, saying:
solitude, solitude, solitude:

you have it at last—your
solitude writing on water,
alone with its failure.

6.

You are there
on the underside of the page,
a blue flower in my Baedeker,

writing on water. I know it.
The paper pulls under my pen,
peaks into waves

running strongly into the horizon.
The emptiness hardens
with balustrades, risers, and levels,

a staircase of Roman
azaleas. I slip on the blood and the ink
toward the exigent bed

of a poet. All is precarious. A maniac
waits on the streets. Nobody listens. What
must I do? I am writing on water,

blazing with failures, ascending,
descending among lovers and trippers.
You are pressing me hard,

under the paper. At Santa Trinità dei Monti
the stairway parts like an
estuary, rises and falls like a fountain.

There is nothing to see but a death-mask, your
room in an island of risers and treads, oddly
gregarious, an invisible hand in the granite.

7.

The tidal salts drain on a living horizon,
leaving a glare on the blemishing
paper. The silence is mortal. Nobody answers.

(*For Joan Hutton Landis*)

V. *BLOCK ISLAND*: After *The Tempest*

Lie here, my art!—PROSPERO

Block Island Crossing

> *What is't? a spirit?*
> *It carries a brave form. But 'tis a spirit.*
> —MIRANDA

Crossing at Point Judith, one feels the world's
doubleness in the walloping stance of the Ferry—
Elisha's marvelous flatiron afloat in the fog
like a prophet's token: the boat and its baggage,
its plucky machinery, its cautionary noises,
swampy or soft-spoken, dividing the watery
flannels without wrinkle or seam, to its destination.

Below, inlanders, islanders. A stable
of station-wagons. The cold-drink and the hamburger
concession with its branding-iron's sizzle
of stabbed bicarbonation, mustard in tumblers
under a gable of bulbs.
                    Outside, the yielding opalescence
and the steam, the nearly visible folding and unfolding
of the spaces, fog in its thermal channels
scudding the levels with a gull's evasions,
flying its semaphore of noises, bell-
clappers, conch-sounds, to a clutter of island pilings.

For suddenly, it is *there*!
                    Somehow, in the drenched
displacement, a boat no bigger than a haddock
asserts its ungainly will to cross, with its gimcrack
universe intact, endures its self-effacement and its loss
and heaves a hawser to the opposite landing.

55

                                    The island
waits, placed and substantial. What was double or indistinct—
the rose-hip and the cranberry and the pure precipitation
that effaced them—merge in a common passion for existence.
Headlands and beaches, the Lighthouse in the middle
distance, open their burning vectors on the water
with a map-maker's precision, circle the air
with soundings to say where the rock was ambiguous,
the ferry's bow and the Village, a single vision.

There is light on the bluffs and light enough in the berry.

We know what the dove knows in our casual
chaos.
        The gangway is down.
                            A mountain dries for us.

(*For Mary Jo Shelly*)

Southeast Lighthouse

> . . . *teach me how*
> *To name the bigger light, and how the less.*
> —CALIBAN

Chaos is always there. The Lighthouse's gesture,
poised on its needle, sweeping a compass's foot
three hundred and sixty degrees in chalk and acetylene,
mapping, unmapping, sowing and scything the air,
erasing the seas, tells us in freezing graffiti:
the chaos is there, it is there.

Night shows us a blind man's cane—light tapping the rocks
of an arranged interior whose dangerous threshhold is fixed
in a salt parabola, so the keel may not utterly drown
in the doorway, the seven white and the eight black blocks
of the headland not suddenly reverse themselves, the watcher
hallucinate and go down

as the furniture of ocean pitches us toward a window
where the slain eye looks at crazy tungsten raking
the zenith with its platinum track, Toledan or Damascene, raw
with the burin's filings—seeing nothing
yet mapping a lane in the brine where Oedipus or Lear
might walk as though they saw:

Saw the ship come unbroken to the pilings, as if
it had learned something of the plummet; saw the skeptical cities
    succumb
in the night of punishing water; saw chaos itself
at last, unmoved by the word of God, while the face
of the deep still looked out of darkness toward a negative
finger, and was dumb.

57

For: *nothing has been created. Nothing. Nothing.* All is yet to come.
The cloud that whirls in the Lighthouse's vector confirms
the superstitious dream of Adam and the geography of danger,
the staggering keel in the shipwreck, the gull's wing bloodying glass.
The ocean spins emptily. The Lighthouse counts three hundred
    and sixty degrees; and the salt
comedy of unknowing begins.

Soundings

I'll drown my book.—PROSPERO

1.

The sea closes like a plum
on its stone. It will presently fall.
Halfway toward Newton's head

it shows a nap of numbers,
rosettes for the navigator,
under the mariner's glass, a gooseflesh of soundings—

a flat map where gulls enter
reading the fine print in tawny aquarelle. Later,
that ripping of edges

at the Lighthouse's base, a pounding
of tumblers and bells in the coarse salt,
the reef in its necklace of skulls.

2.

Whales work. A swan leading its cindery cygnets
sees transparently down
to the center: Alice's tears, the nausea of Rimbaud,

green gall and spittle
to pucker the sea floor, constellate
polyps in the flinty asparagus,

the unsuffocating flora
where the diver's heart explodes
in cross-threads of mica and the sardine throbs like a hummingbird—

all the bright business of darkness
I would read in the charred scrolls, the double pillars
of vellum, crossing with chariots, like Torah.

3.

The parachutists lie where they have fallen
on mandalas of terry cloth. The sea has cast
them up like anemones, split prismatic canvas

in spinnakers of beach umbrellas. A sound
of drowned transistors, gull's claws in the froth,
a lifeguard's whistle, the breathing of pontoons,

hisses through the noon's bicarbonation.
Light hardens the facets; but there in the sleeper's
eye, the glacial emulsions of a camera,

sight keeps its core of darkness—
an apple halved, and, in the satin pockets, point
touching point, like Indian paisley, the seed-shaped tears.

4.

What holds the eye to its salt, Orphean
lookers-back, Sodomites, ruminants
licking a briny meniscus—

what? The pastures of plankton,
coffined nerve-gas, sarcophagi
lifted like thistle three miles under,

are not as inland meadows are. There,
green goes aerial, drives star over star through the chicory,
stays nowhere, asks nothing of the malcontent—but here?

Something unappeasable
in the blond marination of whips, melancholy
bearing night in its bile: an expectation of black.

5.

Failures! The thunderheads of bracken
rise over minefields, the sea burns
like a slum, sends arabesques of oil

on all my summer salvage:
young losses, nightmares, a kneecap smashed,
or a back, forfeiture of sons,

the wild severity of poems,
the mouth's sanctuary, the Mona Lisa smile
of adolescent bellies sloping toward their sex,

drowned fathers, photographs, translations
in the middle kingdom of the languages—
fog, foam, hallucinated form.

6.

Noah's drunken dream: the animals in twos,
delineated water, rainbows. Fog works in the mummy-cloths;
the sandspit goes, in its spiral nebulae of boulders.

the millrace of the upper air, flying
iodine, the binnacle's
mathematics, battlefields of bathers,

the Pharaonic sun that calcifies the beaches
and cuts the swimmer's diamond in the sand,
the light dividing water from the land,

matter, motion, mind—all goes to bandages,
equinoctial steam. The floating bobbins empty,
bearing the corpse of darkness toward the ocean.

7.

Block Island, Black Island;* Pablo, Prospero—
how utterly the landmarks tarnish!
Our "residence on earth" shows spiracles,

watery torches, shark's fins, the purgatorial jaw
of Jonah's disobedience. *It is time
for the breaking of wands and books.*

The rose-hip looses
its petal on the blackberry's dagger
under the certain apparition of a ship,

and I enter the desolating soda
again, taking the whole weight of the sun upon my skin
to drive the darkness in.

(*For Pablo Neruda*)

* Isla Negra—"Black Island": the Pacific retreat of Pablo Neruda.

Freshwater Pond

Where the bee sucks, there suck I.—ARIEL

The parting of waters should make
a swarthier sound than this:
a noise like the breaking of bronzes
in alluvial silt, Rameses'
chariot wheels, the tambourines
of Deborah and Judith,
Armageddons, hosannas—

but here where the wars of bayberry and peat
sweeten the whole of a promontory,
invisible hexagons meet
in a swarming of salts,
driving their honey and gall
through the core of a continent's
fault, to hum like the wax of a hive.

The line of the spit, where the
snapping turtle and monogamous swan
forage for sugar, glares in a jungle
of cattails. No one can say where
the salt of the juggernaut stalls,
or the bland and the bitter cross over
to mesh like the grids of a sieve.

Yet heavily, heavily one way the facets
of brine drop their plummet's weight
in vaults of acidulous bracken
to harden in iron and manganese;
and the other way the sweets in the rose-hip
climb up a thicket of seeds and leaven their wine
on the summit for Ariel's pleasures.

(*For Virginia Carlin*)

A Choppy Sea

All corners else o' th' earth
Let liberty make use of. Space enough
Have I in such a prison.
                    —FERDINAND

The world's containment, provisional
as porcelain or crystal—a cup's
clasp on an abyss,
or the upward look from a gorge
through a fillet of leaves at Andromeda riding the zenith,
Tiepolo's goddesses skewed on a dome's
umbilicus—persuade us we are finite and bring us at length
to an ocean balancing an island like an egg in a spoon.

Shelf over shelf, the continent offers its brim,
gathers in basins and columns,
a rising and falling of wells,
Corinthian water or the pillars of Angkor Vat. Spending
and replenishing itself, the void fills like a bucket,
the ocean creaks and goes taut,
a dipper empties, and the fountains of Genesis
soak their way through the cisterns and blacken the ledges.

The gull sees it with a predator's
excitement: confinement's opposite angel, overplus,
that lives on the thirst of the starved and abstemious.
Over the platter, the pitcher: the pit of the cataract,
the windlass, the trough, and the pail,
the underground spilth of a world that feeds on excess
and shows the way to the depths—
the granaries under the shale and the magnets
that sleep in the forms,
pulling continents, islands, messengers, into the eye of the storm.

But nothing will happen today.

A bather stands on a sandbar feeling the sinister
freeze at his ankles. A sailboat tightens its cloths.
High tide: with a tarry light in the greens.
A foaming of potsherds, anthracite flaking the spray,
Indian arrowheads.

Three forty-five: the ferry is punctual.
$$\text{The pylons yaw}$$
and give way.
$$\text{It is a choppy sea.}$$

Nighttown: Block Island

*Here's neither bush nor shrub to bear any weather at all, and
another storm is brewing.*

—TRINCULO

Nothing will happen today. The clammers
are back from the sand-flats, with crystals of chitin
and silt in the slats of their buckets.

The yachts have gutted their catch in the Basin,
slashed filet and roe from the fishbones and construed
all the entrails. The haruspicies are good.

The lights go out at Ballard's and Baroni's. Trinculo
lies down in his litter of six-packs to dream of banquets and noises.
The adolescents pair off in the lutheran curfew.

The streets stream toward an ocean mapped out with
nautical numbers. In the lattices of porches the Lighthouse's helix
hones its facade of Victorian scrimshaw and gingerbread—

all the banked transportation of bicycles,
boathouses, bell buoys, triangular flags to point
to the weather tomorrow, blind polaroid, sun lotions.

Only the headlands show garnets and blues,
a tunnel of melting graffiti fogged with initials
and gases—submarine, subterranean.

But something is pulling the pylons
askew in the underground cities, gnawing away the foundations.
The plumb lines that fasten the tides to the craters

70

and calculate deserts are tilting a continent's biases.
The oceans are drying to peat on their shelves, the peat into cinder
and flint. Chaos is showing its hearth-bed of iron

again, black holes and barnacles, the fiery maws
of a starving leviathan. In the dark of the morning
a planet is turning to ether, as midwinter landscapes

efface themselves under snow; an island is going
to blubber and fin, a garbage for krakens, streamers
of pitchblende, coronas. There are warnings.

All hangs in the balance. All waits for the
rubbery boots of a swordfisher, a deckhand to fold the drowned
tarpaulins, and open a lane to Portugal.

Ariel comes with his tray for the drunkards
in a thicket of berries and cutlery. Big-bladdered, they stand
to the arch of their urine, caryatids supporting a rainbow; and

nothing will happen today.

Library of Congress Cataloging in Publication Data

Belitt, Ben
    The double witness.

    (Princeton series of contemporary poets)
    I. Title.
PS3552.E48D6   811'.5'4   77-2534
ISBN 0-691-06346-X
ISBN 0-691-01341-1 pbk.